Great Moments
in
Space Exploration

Earth's Journey Through Space
Electromagnetism, and How It Works
Gravity, and How It Works
Great Extinctions of the Past
Great Inventions of the 20th Century
Great Moments in Space Exploration
Volcanic Eruptions, Earthquakes, and Tsunamis
Weather, and How It Works

SCIENTIFIC AMERICAN

Great Moments
in
Space Exploration

By Peter Jedicke

CHELSEA HOUSE
PUBLISHERS
An imprint of Infobase Publishing

Chelsea House
An imprint of Infobase Publishing
132 West 31st Street
New York NY 10001

ISBN-10: 0-7910-9046-9

ISBN-13: 978-0-7910-9046-6

Library of Congress Cataloging-in-Publication Data

Jedicke, Peter.
    Scientific American. Great moments in space exploration / Peter Jedicke.
        p. cm.
    Includes bibliographical references and index.
    ISBN 0-7910-9046-9 (hardcover)
 1. Astronautics—History—Juvenile literature. 2. Outer space—Exploration—
History—Juvenile literature. I. Title. II. Title: Great moments in space
exploration.

    TL793.J4167 2006
    629.409—dc22   2006014774

Chelsea House books are available at special discounts when purchased
in bulk quantities for businesses, associations, institutions, or sales
promotions. Please call our Special Sales Department in New York at
(212) 967-8800 or (800) 322-8755.

You can find Chelsea House on the World Wide Web at
http://www.chelseahouse.com

Series designed by Gilda Hannah
Cover designed by Takeshi Takahashi

Printed in the United States of America

Bang GH 10 9 8 7 6 5 4 3 2 1

This book is printed on acid-free paper.

All links and Web addresses were checked and verified to be correct at
the time of publication. Because of the dynamic nature of the Web, some
addresses and links may have changed since publication and may no
longer be valid.

Contents

CHAPTER ONE

Rockets and Missiles

Have you ever launched a model **rocket** at your school? With proper planning and safety precautions, a long narrow tube with a chemical rocket engine can zoom hundreds of yards into the sky. Modern model rockets are based on the same ideas as the fireworks and weapons that were invented in China centuries ago.

A rocket uses the principle of action and reaction, which Sir Isaac Newton first explained in 1687. Newton said that a force only occurs when one object pushes on another. But since the other object always pushes back on the first, forces always come in pairs. If the two objects are both free to move, they will go in opposite directions. There is really no "reaction" involved, because each object has a direct action on the other. When a rocket is launched, the burning fuel is one object and the rocket itself is the other.

When a model rocket is launched straight up, its speed increases furiously until its fuel runs out. Then, it continues to climb, even though its powered flight has ended. Eventually, of course, it reaches a peak and falls freely back to the ground. The path it follows is called its **trajectory**, and after the fuel is gone, the trajectory is called **ballistic**. If a ballistic rocket is launched on an angle, it can travel a considerable distance on a ballistic trajectory before landing.

KONSTANTIN TSIOLKOVSKY

Konstantin Eduardovich Tsiolkovsky was a boy in Russia in the 1860s, before the time of communism. At the age of nine, he became ill with a disease called scarlet fever and, as a result, became partially deaf. His mother died a few years later, and young Tsiolkovsky had to do all his school work at home, but he enjoyed studying, particularly math and science. At age 16, he visited a university in Moscow and listened to lectures through an ear trumpet.

Tsiolkovsky became a teacher and continued to study physics and chemistry. He realized that liquid fuels released their energy more quickly than solid fuels, such as gunpowder, which were used in cannons and firecrackers. He also understood how the force of burning fuel shoots a rocket forward while the fuel itself is pushed backward. That means a rocket does not need air to hold it up, the way a balloon or a winged glider does.

Tsiolkovsky came up with the idea that a "rocket train" could be built in stages. Each stage

Konstantin Tsiolkovsky, a Russian science teacher, described how rockets could be used for space exploration.

would fire until it ran out of fuel, pushing the entire train forward, and then dropping away until there was only one stage left, which would be traveling very fast. Before he died in 1935, Tsiolkovsky imagined that one day airlines would offer rocket trips from Moscow to Mars. He wrote that "Earth is the cradle of humanity, but one cannot live forever in a cradle." Tsiolkovsky is called "the father of space travel."

Liquid-Fuel Rockets

Robert Goddard fired the first modern rocket using liquid fuels on March 16, 1926, near Auburn, Massachusetts. The flight lasted a mere 2.5 seconds, and the rocket rose only 41 feet (14 m) above a farmer's field, but we could say that the rocket was aimed straight at the stars. Goddard later moved to the wide-open spaces of New Mexico and continued to improve his designs.

Meanwhile, a group of engineers in Germany formed a rocket club and began to work on designs similar to Goddard's. When the German government was looking for ideas for secret weapons to use against the Allies in World War II, the army hired some of the men in the rocket club. The result was a mis-

Many V-2 rockets were brought from Germany at the end of World War II and tested in the New Mexico desert.

sile called the *V-2*. The "V" stood for "vengeance weapon." The engineers worked very hard to make a successful design, and thousands of V-2s were packed with explosives and launched toward Great Britain and other war zones. Sadly, many citizens were killed by V-2 explosions in the summer of 1944.

The Race Is On

When World War II ended the following year, the United States Army captured some of the German scientists and their equipment. The U.S. Army had never asked Goddard to work with them. They now realized they had missed a huge opportunity to develop advanced weapons. Under contract with the U.S. Army, the German scientists began a development program in the New Mexico desert, cooperating with U.S. rocket scientists. They

ROBERT GODDARD

One day in 1899, young Robert Hutchings Goddard climbed a cherry tree to trim some of its dead branches. It was fall, and Goddard was inspired by the beautiful New England scenery to think of faraway places—even the planet Mars. Wouldn't it be wonderful, Goddard thought, to find some way to travel there?

In high school, he was a popular student who wanted to be successful in math and science. He had to work very hard in school because he suffered from tuberculosis, a disease that often made it hard for him to breathe. He was absent a lot, and it took two extra years before he finally graduated in 1904. When he finished high school, he gave a speech at the commencement ceremony and said, "It is difficult to say what is impossible, for the dream of yesterday is the hope of today and the reality of tomorrow."

Goddard became the first rocket scientist. He experimented with the delicate plumbing necessary to feed liquid fuels into a combustion chamber, where they could burn furiously. He came up with the idea of packing a small parachute into his rockets so that they would land gently instead of crashing. That way he could reuse them and save money. Goddard is called "the father of modern rocketry."

This atomic bomb was one of twenty-four test explosions that took place in the Nevada desert in 1957.

started with test firings of the rockets brought from Germany. Eventually, the rocket program moved to Huntsville, Alabama, and the scientists learned to build new and better rockets like the *Corporal,* the *Redstone,* and the *Atlas.*

However, the *V-2* and the *Redstone* could launch whatever they carried—their **payload**—a few hundred miles or perhaps a few thousand at most. As development continued, it was inevitable that rockets would become an important part of military strategy.

The former Soviet Union had also captured some of the German scientists and equipment. They carried out their own research secretly throughout the 1950s. At the same time, both the United States and the former Soviet Union made rapid progress in the development of **nuclear weapons**. Knowing that the fearsome power unleashed by atomic bombs could be delivered around the world without warning in mere minutes, the two nations became locked in a secret and deadly competition. The political tension that resulted was called the Cold War because, fortunately, neither side ever attacked the other.

Weapons experts in the United States concentrated on making their atomic bombs smaller, so that less powerful rockets could launch them. The researchers in the former Soviet Union worked on more powerful rockets that could carry their heavier bombs. By the mid-1950s, it was obvious that both sides in the Cold War had rockets strong enough to launch payloads other than bombs into space. Humanity stood on the threshold of a new age.

CHAPTER TWO

Satellites

One of the most dramatic moments of the twentieth century occurred on October 4, 1957. The former Soviet Union, using an R-7 Semiorka rocket built for its weapons program, sent a small shiny sphere with four long antennas into space. They called it *Sputnik I. Sputnik* is a Russian word that means "traveling companion." The satellite traveled so fast that its ballistic flight continued all the way around Earth. A radio transmitter on board sent a simple beeping signal that could be heard everywhere as it passed overhead. It was an artificial moon.

Any satellite—natural or artificial—travels in a path called an **orbit**. The same thing applies to the planets of our solar system: they all orbit the Sun. Because outer space is a vacuum with nothing to slow down the moons and planets, they keep orbiting forever. The most important influence on their motion is the force of gravity. In the seventeenth century, along with the laws of force, Sir Isaac Newton also explained how gravity works: It is a force of attraction between any two objects in the universe. Larger objects have stronger forces, and the closer two objects are, the stronger is the force between them. Newton figured out a formula to calculate the strength and direction of the force.

A satellite such as *Echo I* had to coast at about 4.4 miles per second (7 km/sec) to stay in orbit above Earth.

Orbit Calculations

The science of **celestial mechanics** is based on Newton's formula. Moons and planets and even artificial satellites like *Sputnik* move according to the principles of celestial mechanics. If a spaceship travels around Earth with just the right speed in just the right direction, its orbit will be a perfect circle. It will always remain at the same height above Earth and always travel at the same speed. That speed will carry it around Earth in a definite time period.

A spaceship in a different orbit, higher above Earth, will have a much larger circle to travel. Every altitude corresponds to a definite orbital speed. Higher orbits require less speed, though the launch is more difficult because the spaceship has to reach a greater altitude before it begins to circle Earth.

However, most spaceships are not sent into circular orbits. Instead, a spaceship's orbit will have a high point, called **apogee**, and a low point, called **perigee**, and the shape of the orbit will be an ellipse instead of a circle. As the satellite travels around, it will speed up as it approaches perigee, just as it would speed up

CLARKE ORBIT

If an artificial satellite is in a circular orbit 22,240 miles (35,784 km) above Earth, its speed will carry it around the world in almost exactly 24 hours. So, if the orbit is aligned with the equator, it will seem to hover motionless above a particular spot as Earth turns underneath, also in almost exactly 24 hours. Such a "geosynchronous" orbit is a perfect arrangement for aiming an antenna at the satellite. The antenna can be locked in place instead of requiring a complicated apparatus to make it move.

Sir Arthur Charles Clarke, a British radio engineer, figured this out in the 1940s. He realized that a signal transmitted by a satellite in such an orbit could be

The *Vanguard 2* satellite was launched from Cape Canaveral in 1959 on a mission to look down at Earth's clouds.

received by antennas over a very wide area on the ground, almost a third of the entire world. This was the beginning of communications satellites, which are a billion-dollar industry today. There are dozens of satellites at the proper height, and such an orbit is called a **Clarke orbit**.

Clarke had many innovative ideas about space travel and included them in some very imaginative science fiction novels, such as *A Fall of Moondust*, *Rendezvous with Rama*, and *2001: A Space Odyssey*, which was made into a famous movie.

Wernher von Braun, the German-born rocket engineer, led NASA's rocket development in the early 1960s.

if it were falling all the way to the ground. After perigee, the satellite slows down until it reaches apogee. The orbit of *Sputnik I* initially had a 587-mile (939-km) apogee and a 134-mile (215-km) perigee, and it took about 96 minutes to travel around Earth.

Because the Soviet rocket program was so secret, scientists and politicians in the United States were surprised by *Sputnik*. They feared the Soviet Union might be developing other secret projects. A huge effort to catch up began, and it even included building new facilities in schools so young people could learn more science and mathematics to better prepare for the space age.

The former Soviet Union launched many more *Sputniks* and other Earth-orbiting satellites, with names like *Molniya* and *Cosmos,* over the years. The United States' first satellite was *Explorer 1,* which was sent into orbit on February 1, 1958. In that same year, the U.S. government set up the National Aeronautics and Space Administration (**NASA**) to explore outer space. Other notable satellites launched by the United States included *Vanguard, Echo, Syncom*, and *Landsat*. The European Space Agency, China, India, and other countries have also launched their own satellites. The many uses of satellites include relaying data, transmitting navigation signals, military surveillance, observing the surface of Earth, following the movement of storms and other weather features, and scientific research.

So many satellites are orbiting Earth that you will probably see at least one, about as bright as an average star, moving among the constellations, if you pay attention during the first hour of darkness on any clear night of the year. In fact, companies that build and operate satellite services are now a $100-billion-per-year-industry around the globe.

CHAPTER THREE

The Beginnings of Human Spaceflight

Take a deep breath, and then take another. Think about the precious atmosphere that we live in—with its 21% oxygen and 78% nitrogen—which makes life possible and shields us from ultraviolet rays. Think about gravity, which holds you safe against Earth and makes it easy to find things that you put on the table yesterday. Think about rain and clouds, rivers and oceans, always recycling the water that you need.

Now imagine going to a place where none of those things can be taken for granted. Space is almost a perfect vacuum, so you need to bring air and water with you. You need to protect yourself from solar flares and other forms of radiation. Although there is gravity everywhere, it doesn't hold you down in space because you are always falling freely once your rocket motors are turned off. As a result, in space, it's an adventure just sitting still.

First Person to Orbit Earth

That's what the first space travelers did: they sat in a cramped capsule and went along for the ride. When the former Soviet Union launched Yuri Gagarin into orbit in *Vostok I* on April 12, 1961, the flight lasted just one orbit—about 90 minutes. The

Yuri Gagarin's high school mathematics teacher piloted a fighter plane for the former Soviet Union in World War II. Perhaps Gagarin's enthusiasm for flying was inspired by that teacher, because Gagarin started training to become a pilot in the Soviet air force in 1955. Bold, courageous, and hard working, Gagarin was one of twenty-one pilots who were selected five years later as the first cosmonauts. Even among other skilled pilots, Gagarin had an excellent reputation and was voted by his comrade cosmonauts as the best choice to become the first human being in outer space. It also helped that he was 5 feet, 2 inches (158 cm) tall, because there was not much room in the Vostok spacecraft.

Yuri Gagarin returns triumphant, after orbiting Earth.

Standing at the launch pad just before climbing into *Vostok 1*, Gagarin said to the scientists and workers, "In a few minutes a powerful space vehicle will carry me into the distant realm of space. Could one dream of anything greater? It is a responsibility toward all mankind, toward its present and future." Engineers locked his controls so that he couldn't push a wrong button in space, but he reported that being weightless didn't cause him any difficulty. On **re-entry**, he parachuted out of the capsule and landed in a field where a lady was planting potatoes. "Have you come from outer space?" she asked him, and indeed he had.

When his fellow cosmonaut Vladimir Komarov was killed in *Soyuz 1*, Gagarin wrote: "Nothing will stop us. The road to the stars is steep and dangerous." Gagarin himself was killed in a fighter jet crash in bad weather on March 27, 1968. He was only 44 years old.

United States responded a few months later by launching Alan Bartlett Shepard, Jr., in a Mercury capsule on a Redstone rocket that couldn't even reach the speed required to make orbit. Shepard got to the edge of space and then was fished out of the Atlantic Ocean after just 15 minutes in flight. In those days, it was an enormous challenge even to build a small spaceship that could carry a person into space and back right away.

However, the greatest thing about human technology is that we improve as we learn and gain more and more experience. In the Mercury program there were 19 unmanned launches to test the various systems! Step by step, the designers and engineers in both the former Soviet Union and the United States solved every little problem and built more reliable spaceships. John Herschel Glenn, Jr., was the first U.S. **astronaut** in orbit, almost a year after Gagarin, in a Mercury capsule he named *Friendship 7*. Glenn

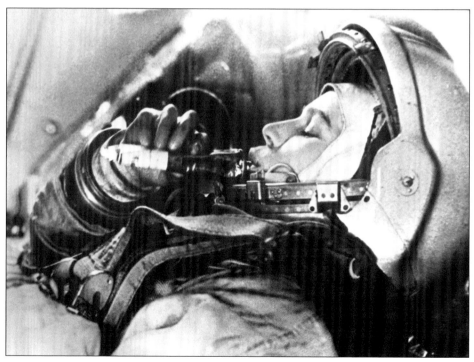

Valentina Tereshkova practices eating space food in a training suit before spending three days in orbit.

The first U.S. astronaut to fly outside a space capsule was Edward H. White in 1965.

stayed up for three orbits of Earth. Although Glenn had many minor problems, such as keeping cool in his spacesuit and responding to a signal that said his heat shield might come loose, none of them prevented a safe landing in the Atlantic Ocean. The distance he traveled in only five hours was almost 76,000 miles (122,000 km).

People across the United States were thrilled by Glenn's success, and NASA followed it with three more orbital Mercury flights. Meanwhile, the former Soviet Union also made strides in its program. There were five more Vostok and two Voskhod flights. Valentina Vladimirovna Tereshkova became the first woman in space on board *Vostok 6,* and Alexei Archipovich Leonov made the first spacewalk during the *Voskhod 2* mission.

More Ambitious Projects

After Mercury, the United States began the Gemini program. A more powerful rocket, the Titan, was used, and the larger capsule was fitted with maneuvering rockets so that the spaceship could change its orbit slightly. Hardly luxurious, the Gemini spacecraft nevertheless could support two astronauts for up to fourteen days, as on *Gemini 7*. The overall goals of the Gemini missions were to demonstrate the technology and to practice the skills needed to go to the Moon. These included **docking** with a booster rocket and performing basic tasks outside the space capsule. The 10 manned Gemini flights included more than 600 orbits of Earth without any major failures. NASA engineers declared that they were ready to move on to the Apollo program, which would involve three astronauts.

The former Soviet Union was also developing missions for three space travelers. Their next spacecraft was called *Soyuz*, which means "union" in Russian. At first, the new program was plagued with failure. But just like the NASA engineers in the early 1960s, the Soviet engineers in the late 1960s kept working on the problems, and they solved them one by one. With many modifications and variations, the Soyuz design is still being used in the opening years of the twenty-first century.

THE PRICE OF AMBITION

Three U.S. astronauts and four Soviet cosmonauts lost their lives in spacecraft accidents that occurred during the early days of space travel.

DATE	MISSION	WE REMEMBER
Jan. 27, 1967	*Apollo 1* (fire in capsule during prelaunch test)	Virgil "Gus" Grissom Roger Chaffee Edward H. White
Apr. 24, 1967	*Soyuz 1* (parachute failure)	Vladimir Komarov
June 30, 1971	*Soyuz 11* (lost breathing air during re-entry)	Vladislav Volkov Georgi Dobrovolski Viktor Patsaev

CHAPTER FOUR

The Moon Landings

John Fitzgerald Kennedy was youthful and handsome and belonged to a famous, wealthy New England family. In 1961, he was also president of the United States. Citizens admired him, and his leadership spawned a nationwide mood of optimism. In response to *Sputnik,* there were new initiatives in education and science across the United States. Although Shepard's flight in the Mercury program was not as impressive as the mission of Yuri Gagarin a few weeks earlier, the U.S. space program was obviously poised for greater achievements.

Kennedy and his government decided the time was right to announce a new project that would rank among the most ambitious in human history. On May 25, 1961, Kennedy stood before Congress and said, "This nation should commit itself to achieving the goal . . . of landing a man on the moon and returning him safely to the Earth." Kennedy set a deadline of 1970 to accomplish this enormous feat. With this commitment, an amazing adventure began.

The Development of a Moon Rocket

The idea of sending a human being to the Moon goes back thousands of years, but no one took it seriously, even just a short while before Kennedy's speech. NASA had a vague plan, code-named Apollo, as a starting point. Wernher von Braun's team was working on a rocket called the *Saturn V* (where the "V" is the Roman numeral "5," not a letter) that would be 10 times more powerful than anything yet built. NASA now asked: Could the *Saturn V* be used for a moon shot?

Science fiction writers had long imagined a rocket that could lift off from Earth, go directly to the Moon, land, and come back. But that would mean taking the entire weight of the fuel tanks all the way there, even after they were mostly empty! Not even the *Saturn V* could lift a manned spaceship to the Moon like that. So, to save weight, fuel, and money, the engineers came up with a mission plan called Lunar Orbit **Rendezvous** (LOR). The trick was to take a second, lightweight craft to the Moon and leave it

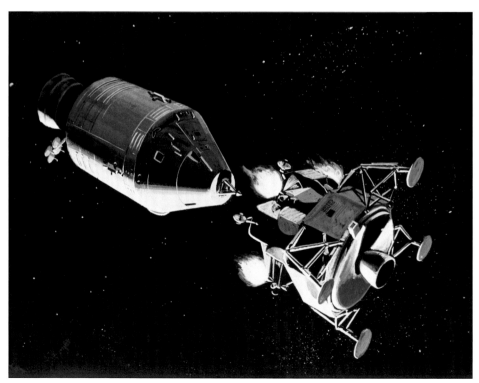

An artist's illustration shows the Apollo Command and Service Module separating from the Lunar Module.

A majestic night launch from Cape Canaveral lifted *Apollo 17* on its final mission to the Moon.

there. That way the main ship, called the Command Module, wouldn't have to lift itself off the surface of the Moon. The lander, or Lunar Module (LM), wouldn't need to be strong enough to make a fiery re-entry through Earth's atmosphere. Only two astronauts would venture to the surface of the Moon, leaving their shipmate in the Command Module to orbit the Moon and wait for their return.

Apollo: To the Moon

NASA worked on building the Apollo program even while the Mercury and Gemini missions were still flying. Even after a terri-

Buzz Aldrin, the second person on the Moon, takes the last step off the ladder of the Lunar Module.

ble disaster during a simulated launch test of *Apollo 1*, NASA stayed on target to meet Kennedy's deadline. Although there were rumors that the Soviet space program was also in the race to the Moon, we now know that the Soviet designers were not progressing fast enough to win. Step by step, the first Apollo missions—unmanned as well as manned—proved that the complicated hardware worked.

Finally, on July 16, 1969, all was ready. The mission was called *Apollo 11,* and the astronauts were Neil Armstrong, "Buzz" Aldrin, and Michael Collins. At the top of the 363-foot (111-m) moon rocket was an escape rocket that could lift the Command Module to safety if something went wrong during the launch. Then, came the Command Module itself, about the size of a walk-in closet. Most of the Command Module's fuel and supplies were behind it in a Service Module. Below that, the Lunar Module was stored, with its spindly legs folded, inside a tapered shroud. All of this weighed less than 2% of the whole moon rocket. *Apollo 11* rode on top of a *Saturn V* with almost 6,600,000 pounds (3,000,000 kg) of fuel inside. It thundered through the clear blue sky over the coast of Florida.

THE MANNED APOLLO MISSIONS

MISSION	LAUNCH DATE	ASTRONAUTS
Apollo 7	Oct. 11, 1968	Wally Schirra, Donn Eisele, Walter Cunningham
Apollo 8	Dec. 21, 1968	Frank Borman, Jim Lovell, William Anders
Apollo 9	Mar. 3, 1969	Jim McDivitt, David Scott, "Rusty" Schweickart
Apollo 10	May 18, 1969	Tom Stafford, John W. Young, Eugene Cernan
Apollo 11	July 16, 1969	Neil Armstrong*, "Buzz" Aldrin*, Michael Collins
Apollo 12	Nov. 14, 1969	Pete Conrad*, Alan Bean*, Richard Gordon
Apollo 13	Apr. 11, 1970	Jim Lovell, Fred Haise, Jack Swigert
Apollo 14	Jan. 31, 1971	Alan Shepard*, Ed Mitchell*, Stuart Roosa
Apollo 15	Jul. 26, 1971	David Scott*, Jim Irwin*, Al Worden
Apollo 16	Apr. 16, 1972	John W. Young*, Charlie Duke*, "Ken" Mattingly
Apollo 17	Dec. 7, 1972	Eugene Cernan*, Harrison "Jack" Schmitt*, Ron Evans

* walked on the Moon

While on the way to the Moon, the Command Module and Service Module turned around and linked nose to nose with the Lunar Module. Three days later, the astronauts were in orbit around the Moon. They spent a few hours checking out their systems. Then, Armstrong and Aldrin climbed into the Lunar Module and rode it down to the surface, standing at the controls and looking out the window at the drab, gray ground. On July 20, 1969, humans first set foot on another body in space. With television cameras beaming their moonwalk back home, Armstrong and Aldrin planted a U.S. flag, set up an experiment to measure

During the Apollo 17 mission, astronauts checked out this large boulder in the Moon's Taurus-Littrow Valley.

moonquakes, gathered 48 pounds (22 kg) of rock samples, took dozens of pictures, and talked to President Richard Nixon from Washington. After spending less than a day on the Moon, they blasted off, rejoined Collins in the Command Module, and flew safely home.

NASA planned to continue the Apollo project with at least six more moon missions. All except *Apollo 13* made it to the Moon's surface. In a way, *Apollo 13* was successful, too, because, after a small explosion blew open their Service Module, NASA engineers figured out how to get the astronauts back alive. Despite the successes, the U.S. government stopped funding Apollo, and equipment for the seventh, eighth, and ninth moon missions was used for other projects.

Moon Rocks

Data from the Apollo adventure has kept scientists busy for a generation. After studying the 840 pounds (382 kg) of samples brought back by the astronauts, scientists concluded that the Moon split off from Earth about 4.5 billion years ago, when a very large **asteroid** collided with Earth. Almost none of the iron from Earth's core was torn out, which is why the Moon has very little iron and is only 60% as dense as Earth overall. Small quantities of radioactive oxygen in the moon rocks match the amount of radioactive oxygen in Earth rocks.

Mainly because of heat from the collision, the Moon's surface was almost completely covered by oceans of molten lava for a hundred million years or so. Slightly heavier rocks sank through the molten lava as the less heavy rocks solidified. When the Moon's surface was almost cooled, the last volcanoes forced some of the slightly heavier rocks back up to the surface. Unlike Earth, the Moon did cool right through and no longer has a molten core. Since the time the lava turned solid, the only thing that has happened on the surface of the Moon has been a hail of various-sized asteroids and meteoroids that came crashing down. That is, until 12 brave men left footprints in the shallow dust.

CHAPTER FIVE

Robots to the Inner Solar System

Space travel is dangerous. By far the safest way to explore space is to stay home and send the best cameras and scientific instruments we can build to gather all the important data we need. It has even been suggested that we should never send any humans into space at all! After all, if we give scientists good pictures of some faraway place, they can tell us an awful lot about what that place is like.

Steps to the Moon

The first obvious place to send a space probe was the Moon. It's only 238,855 miles (384,400 km) away, so both NASA and the former Soviet Union launched unmanned lunar missions in the 1960s. *Luna 3* was first to send photographs of the back side of the moon, which we cannot see with telescopes from Earth. Probes from the United States named *Ranger 6*, *Ranger 7*, and *Ranger 8* took a total of 17,267 pictures before they each smashed on the Moon. These pictures confirmed that there were thousands of craters too small to be seen clearly from Earth.

After 1976, no human instruments were sent to the moon until Japan became the third country to explore our neighbor by sending a spacecraft named *Hiten* there. It was put in orbit around the Moon in 1992. The United States has sent two spacecraft to the Moon since then, including *Clementine,* which found evidence of ice in craters near the Moon's South Pole, and *Lunar Prospector.* In fact, NASA has made all 1,800,000 images taken by *Clementine* available on the Internet as a virtual map of the entire lunar surface! The European Space Agency also sent a probe, called *SMART-1*, to orbit the Moon. It began taking close-up pictures in 2005.

Beyond the Moon

One surprising thing about launching rockets across the solar system is that most of the rocket's fuel is used just getting away from Earth. Science fiction author Robert A. Heinlein wrote: "Once you're in Earth orbit, you're halfway to anywhere." This is not only because of Earth's strong gravity but also because Earth is moving at 19 miles per second (30 km per second) in its orbit around the Sun. Any spacecraft going to another planet already has that much speed as soon as it leaves Earth. To get to Venus, second planet from the Sun, a spaceship actually has to slow down to 17.2 miles per second (27.5 km per second). The spaceship will then fall downward toward the Sun in a long loop, speeding up as it falls and meeting Venus in about five months. When the spaceship gets there, it will have to slow down a little more to match orbits with Venus.

Voyages to Venus

From 1961 to 1983, the former Soviet Union launched a number of probes toward Venus. Most were named Venera. With its sulfuric acid clouds and boiling-hot temperatures, Venus is a tremendous challenge for spacecraft. Many of the 19 Soviet missions failed, but *Venera 4* was the first spaceship to enter the atmosphere of another planet; *Venera 7* was the first to land on another planet; and *Venera 9* transmitted the first photographs from the surface of another planet. The last two Venera probes

Most of the famous robot space probes were built at one place—the Jet Propulsion Laboratory (JPL) in Pasadena, California. Today, more than 5,000 scientists and technicians work there in a vast complex of buildings and workshops, but JPL started in a dusty, dry riverbed below the San Gabriel Mountains. In the 1930s, Theodore von Kármán and his students from the nearby California Institute of Technology launched small, experimental rockets there. When the United States Army wanted to find a way to help heavy airplanes take off from short runways, they hired the students to study the idea of propelling a jet by rockets. The technique was called Jet-Assisted Take-Off, or JATO. That's how JPL got started.

When NASA was put in charge of all space travel in 1958, JPL was working with the Army to build simple satellites. The entire project was transferred to NASA. JPL continued to develop unmanned space probes, and their reputation has been growing ever since. Once a year, JPL has an open house so that young people and their parents can visit the laboratories and see how real rocket science works.

In the Jet Proplusion Laboratory, scientists wearing 3D glasses peer at a large stereo map of Venus, which is based on radar data from the *Magellan* spacecraft.

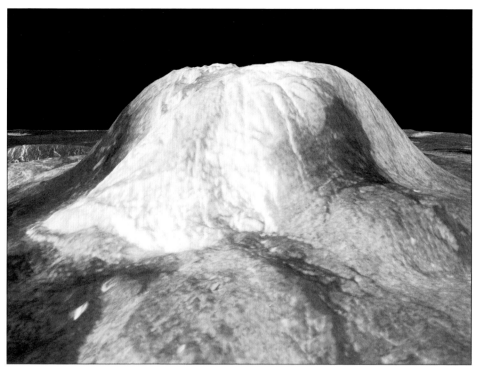

Using radar data from the *Magellan* spacecraft, a computer generated this image of Gula Mons, a volcano on Venus.

were renamed *Vega* and included instruments that continued on to view Halley's comet.

The United States also sent three Mariners and two Pioneer missions to Venus. *Mariner 2* was the first spaceship to fly by another planet at close range. In 1974, *Mariner 10* zoomed past Venus on its way to three encounters with the planet Mercury. *Mariner 10* discovered that Mercury is completely covered by craters, like the Moon. A five-year **radar**-mapping mission called Magellan was also sent to Venus. The *Magellan* probe showed us that there were once many large volcanoes on Venus.

Missions to Mars

Perhaps the most fascinating target for space probes has been the planet Mars. Often the closest planet to Earth, Mars has a thin, cold, and dry atmosphere and a rocky, desertlike surface. The first mission to fly by Mars was *Mariner 4,* a U.S. project, in 1965. The pictures it took showed that the landscape of Mars also has many craters. There were none of the canals that some observers thought they saw from Earth, but it turned out that dust storms

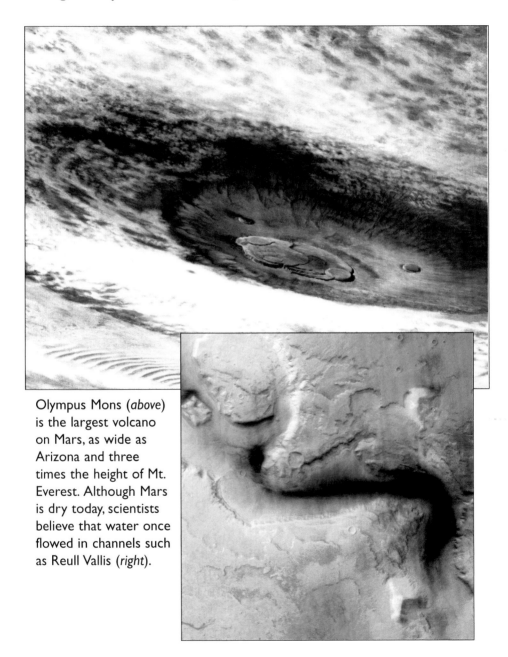

Olympus Mons (*above*) is the largest volcano on Mars, as wide as Arizona and three times the height of Mt. Everest. Although Mars is dry today, scientists believe that water once flowed in channels such as Reull Vallis (*right*).

in the Martian atmosphere hid many interesting features from *Mariner 4.* A few years later, *Mariner 9* was the first spaceship to orbit another planet, and it discovered both a canyon 2,500 miles (4,000 km) long on Mars and Olympus Mons, the largest mountain in the Solar System. There were also dry riverbeds that made it look like water had once flowed on Mars—but there was no sign of any water today.

Many of the projects devoted to Mars were twin spacecraft, one to land on the surface and the other to orbit the planet. None of the Soviet Union's missions were completely successful. Neither was the *Nozomi* probe, sent by Japan, or the *Beagle 2* lander from the European Space Agency (ESA). But NASA's *Viking 1* and *Viking 2* twin probes in 1976 succeeded, returning a wealth of data about the atmosphere and the soil. In the 1990s, the United States also sent *Sojourner,* a lander, and *Pathfinder,* a small, wheeled robot that rolled away from *Sojourner.*

Even more amazing results have come from the two rovers, named *Spirit* and *Opportunity,* which made their way to Mars in January 2004. They traveled thousands of yards across the landscape and even discovered a meteorite lying on the surface! Interesting small rocks, nicknamed **blueberries**, were also discovered. They almost certainly prove there was once a lot of water on Mars. Although none of the spacecraft that landed on Mars have found any evidence of life there, finding out where the water went may yet reveal some wonderful secrets. Then, in 2005, ESA's *Mars Express* orbiter took a lovely photograph showing a small lake in a crater—water—but frozen solid. A future mission will drill below the surface to look for water that might be frozen and mixed in with the soil.

CHAPTER SIX

Robots to the Outer Solar System

In 1965, Gary Flandro was a student at the California Institute of Technology. While doing a summer project on the topic of space travel, he realized that the giant planets Jupiter, Saturn, Uranus, and Neptune were all coming around to the same side of the Solar System. This meant that a spaceship could use the gravity of each planet to pull it along, speeding it to the next planet. It would take less than half as much time to visit all four planets as anyone had previously calculated. Flandro called this the "Grand Tour," and his summer project became part of NASA's plan to explore the outer planets in the 1970s.

Pioneer and Voyager

Four unmanned spacecraft were sent past the giant planets, two Pioneers and two in the Mariner series. *Pioneer 10* and *Pioneer 11* were launched in 1973. *Pioneer 10* sent back the first close-up pictures of Jupiter's cloud systems, with its storms so big that they would cover the entire Pacific Ocean. Since then, *Pioneer 10* has been headed out of the Solar System. Its power fading, it continued to send data about deep space and was last heard from in

Voyager 1 space probe took this dramatic photo of Jupiter's cloud formations and the moons Io and Europa.

2003. Meanwhile, *Pioneer 11* swung by Jupiter on its way to Saturn, giving us our first detailed views of the famous rings. *Pioneer 11* is also on a trajectory out of the Solar System, but, since 1995, Earth has been out of range of its antenna.

The Mariner ships had more powerful instruments and bigger cameras than the trailblazing Pioneers. Before launch in 1977, the Mariners were renamed *Voyager 1* and *Voyager 2*. Within a few days of approaching Jupiter, *Voyager 1* took some of the most surprising pictures ever seen. They showed that Jupiter's moon Io (pronounced EYE-oh) was not a dead and dormant orb like our Moon. Instead, Io is covered with recent lava, and huge, new volcanoes are constantly erupting!

Voyager 1 went on to Saturn. Its target there was the moon Titan, which is the only moon with a thick atmosphere. Pictures from *Voyager 1* showed that the atmosphere is thick enough to shroud the surface from view. Aiming for Titan meant that *Voyager 1* could not get the proper gravity boost from Saturn to continue the Grand Tour. So, *Voyager 1*'s path took it out of the solar system without going near Uranus and Neptune.

Voyager 2 visited all the giant planets—the only spacecraft to realize the complete Grand Tour. After taking fabulous photo-

CARL SAGAN

Perhaps the most famous scientist in North America in the 1970s and 1980s was Carl Edward Sagan. As professor at Cornell University, he studied the atmospheres and the geology of planets. According to Sagan, robot spacecraft were the best way to explore the Solar System. Sagan also convinced other scientists that it was worth studying the idea that life might exist on another planet, even if the possibility were remote.

The books he wrote, such as *The Cosmic Connection* and *Pale Blue Dot*, were very popular. He also hosted a television series called *Cosmos,* and was well known for saying "billions and billions." The movie *Contact* was based on a novel that Sagan wrote. He inspired many young people to learn about science and study astronomy.

Carl Sagan was a respected scientific researcher, as well as a television personality and a popular writer.

This artist's illustration shows the *Huygens* probe descending through the atmosphere of Saturn's moon, Titan, in 2005.

graphs of Jupiter and its moons in 1979, then of Saturn and its moons in 1981, *Voyager 2* went on to Uranus in 1986 and Neptune in 1989. Pictures showed subtle details in the planets' clouds, as well as dramatic features on their families of rocky and icy moons.

Like the plucky little Pioneers, both Voyagers are traveling so fast that the Sun's gravity can never stop them. Their power supplies should be fine until at least the year 2020, so scientists still have many years of data to look forward to from deep space. Already many billions of miles from home, neither the Pioneers nor the Voyagers are aimed at any nearby stars. But they will con-

Even in a small telescope, the planet Saturn looks as gorgeous as this photo taken by a Voyager space probe.

tinue on as citizens of the galaxy forever. Who knows what adventures lay ahead for them?

The Next Steps

Meanwhile, there have been three other missions beyond the inner solar system. The *Ulysses* space probe, a joint project of NASA and ESA, veered by Jupiter and was sent on a long orbit over the North Pole and South Pole of the Sun. Its task is to study the rays and particles, such as the solar wind, that the Sun sends through the Solar System. The mission will continue until at least the year 2008.

In the 1990s, the *Galileo* spacecraft went on an amazing tour. First it flew past Venus to get a boost in speed and went past Earth for even more speed. Then, in 1991, *Galileo* took the first close-up pictures of an asteroid when it passed by (951) Gaspra.

Not surprisingly, the asteroid was shaped like a potato and covered with small craters. *Galileo* continued on with another pass near Earth and then encountered asteroid (243) Ida in 1993. A

WHERE A ROBOT SPACESHIP GETS ITS POWER

A spacecraft needs energy not only for propulsion but also to power its electronic circuits and mechanical systems. For spaceships near Earth, engineers usually put solar cells in their designs to generate electricity, but once a spaceship goes beyond Mars, even the shining Sun cannot provide enough power for a spaceship to operate. Instead, all the spacecraft that have been sent to Jupiter and beyond have a **radioisotope thermoelectric generator** (RTG).

An RTG uses plutonium-238 as fuel. Although radioactive, plutonium-238 cannot explode like a nuclear bomb. But the radioactivity turns into heat, and the heat activates special electronic circuits called thermocouples. After a few decades, the **thermocouples** get used up and produce too little electricity to power the spacecraft. However, the energy in plutonium-238 lasts a long time—less than half of it is gone after 90 years! RTGs used to power spacecraft are about the size of a backyard barbecue. Tested on military satellites in the 1960s, they were the most obvious choice to power missions to deep space.

The *Galileo* spacecraft, four times the height of a human, was tested at the Jet Propulsion Laboratory in California before launch.

small satellite asteroid was discovered around (243) Ida. The following year, the *Galileo* spacecraft was perfectly positioned to watch comet Shoemaker/Levy 9 plow into Jupiter's atmosphere. Soon after that success, *Galileo* fired its rocket engines and went into orbit around Jupiter. After almost eight years of studying the atmosphere and moons of Jupiter, Galileo was commanded to rocket into the atmosphere and burn up.

In 2004, a probe called *Cassini* arrived at Saturn and went into orbit there. *Cassini* also carried a smaller probe, named *Huygens,* which was built by ESA. *Huygens* dropped down to the surface of Titan and sent back the first data from a moon of another planet. The pictures show eerie features that might be rivers and lakes of hydrocarbon chemicals. The *Cassini* spacecraft will continue to study the other moons until at least August 2008.

Robots from Earth have visited all of the major planets. These intrepid explorers have revealed so much about the Solar System that we can feel at home beyond our own planet for the first time in history.

CHAPTER SEVEN

The Faraway Universe

The easiest way to explore space is to lie down in your backyard and look up at the stars on a clear, dark night. Human beings have been doing this for thousands of years. But the stars are so far away that your eyes can't gather enough light from them to see them very well. In 1610, Galileo Galilei put small lenses in a tube and looked through it. This was the first time anyone turned a telescope on the sky. Scientists have explored space with bigger and better telescopes ever since.

The History of Telescopes

A telescope works like a huge, extra eye that funnels much more light into your own eye than your eye can gather by itself. There have been many different designs of telescopes, but they all fall into two categories. A **refractor** is a telescope that collects light with a lens at the front and sends the light straight through to other lenses at the back. This is the design that Galileo used almost 400 years ago. With it, he discovered that the Moon has craters, the Sun has spots, and Jupiter has four large moons of its own.

The biggest refractor in the world today has a lens 40 inches (102 cm) across. It was built at the Yerkes Observatory in Wisconsin over a century ago. Large refractors are difficult to build because a large lens will sag under its own weight, spoiling the

Galileo eagerly showed the nobles of Venice what he could see through his refractor telescope 400 years ago.

view. Still, small refractors—not much bigger than Galileo's but with much better quality lenses—are popular for backyard observing today.

The other category of telescope is called a **reflector**. It has a mirror at the back of the telescope to collect the light and send it to other lenses and mirrors either on the back or the side of the telescope. Some reflectors also have an extra lens on the front, but it's still the mirror that collects the light. The big advantage of a reflector is that the mirror can be supported from the back. All of the big telescopes in the world today are reflectors, and they are up to 10 times as wide as the largest refractor.

Surprising Discoveries

William Herschel was looking through a reflector on March 13, 1781, when he saw a small blue dot that surprised him. Although it was just on the verge of being bright enough to see without a telescope, no one had ever recorded it before—it was the planet

William Herschel used this telescope, with a wooden tube and a 19-inch (47-cm) mirror, to make many discoveries.

Uranus. Herschel's discovery made him famous and caused a sensation in astronomy. There were new worlds in the universe to be found!

In the nineteenth century, William Parsons, Third Earl of Rosse, better known as Lord Rosse, built the biggest reflector in the world in Ireland. It was built between two large brick walls and supported by slings of rope. Lord Rosse aimed his telescope at many small, cloudy patches in the sky that astronomers had previously called **nebulas**. Smaller telescopes were not able to see the details in a nebula as well as Lord Rosse's telescope.

There was a lot of debate about the true nature of these faraway objects. But in Lord Rosse's telescope, some of them clearly showed a spiral appearance like the famous nebula in the constellation Andromeda. Eventually astronomers agreed that the spiral nebulas were huge galaxies similar to the Milky Way that we live

The Keck I observatory (*left*) and the NASA Infrared Telescope occupy two of the domes on top of Mauna Kea in Hawaii.

Earth's atmosphere is a real problem for astronomers. First, there are the clouds, of course. Then, air all by itself absorbs some of the light from outer space. The higher up you go, the more the air and the clouds are below you and the better you can see the sky above. Add in the effects of pollution and glare from city lights, and you can understand why big, new observatories are built on high mountains, far from big cities or factories, where the air is thin and dry.

An artist sketched this view of the Hubble Space Telescope in front of an imagined giant black hole.

Even better would be to have telescopes in space. The Hubble Space Telescope (HST) was not the first, but it's the most famous. It has a 95-inch (240 cm) mirror, so it's much bigger than a backyard telescope. Being above the atmosphere is what makes the HST so special. But there are dozens of observatories on mountaintops that have bigger telescopes than HST. It

The Hubble Space Telescope took this stunning snapshot of a gas cloud illuminated by the outburst of a star in 2002.

was named after Edwin Hubble, the astronomer who first measured the expansion of the universe.

in, and that they were much farther away than the stars that we can see with our unaided eye.

More exciting discoveries about the Milky Way and other galaxies followed in the twentieth century. Harlow Shapley found that the Solar System is in one of the spiral arms of the Milky Way, not near the center. Edwin Powell Hubble measured the motion of galaxies outside the Milky Way and shocked astronomers, in 1929, with the news that all the galaxies in the universe are rushing away from each other. This means that the entire universe is expanding. Recently, light from even more distant galaxies showed that the age of the universe is about 13,700,000,000 years old. The universe began in an awesome explosion called the **big bang**, and the echoes of that explosion have been observed.

Glass Giants

Throughout the 1950s and 1960s, the biggest telescope in the world was the Hale Telescope on Mount Palomar in California, with its 200-inch (5-m) mirror. Since the beginning of the 1990s, improvements in technology and especially in computers have made it possible to build a new generation of large telescopes. Some, such as Subaru, in Hawaii, and the two Gemini telescopes, one in Hawaii, the other in Chile, are built with a single mirror like the classic reflector design. The Large Binocular Telescope even has two large mirrors.

Others, such as the twin Keck telescopes in Hawaii and the Great Telescope of the Canary Islands, use dozens of six-sided mirror segments that fit together in a tight honeycomb pattern. Even though each individual segment is not too large to manage, the combination is equivalent to a single mirror about 400 inches (10 m) across. New telescopes like these will help astronomers explore space for decades to come.

CHAPTER EIGHT

Habitats in Space

Once human explorers have blazed the way, living in space will certainly follow. Building a space habitat is a tremendous challenge, starting with the need for very powerful rockets that could lift much more than just a manned space capsule or an unmanned robot probe. Imagine having to carry your house up a mountain 230 miles (370 km) high—and then to throw it so hard that it was moving almost 5 miles per second (8,000 m per second)! A large space habitat would have to be assembled from many modules that would be launched separately and would never land on Earth again. Astronauts would have to travel to and from the space station in other vehicles.

Early Designs

Beginning in 1952, Wernher von Braun and Chesley Knight Bonestell, Jr., sketched an early dream of living in giant structures in space in magazine articles. They drew a space station shaped like a huge bicycle wheel, bigger than a sports stadium, with just a few spokes and a large central hub where spaceships could dock. By slowly spinning, these habitats could create a realistic illusion of gravity for folks living inside.

This computer art of a space station is similar to the 1950s designs by Chesley Bonestell, Jr., and Werner von Braun.

In the 1970s, Gerard Kitchen O'Neill calculated how many resources would be required to build a city in space, in the shape of cylinder, a mile (1,600 m) long. There would be room inside for a million people. O'Neill suggested that the space citizens could sell energy back to Earth by collecting sunlight with enormous solar cells and beaming **microwaves** back to antennas on the ground. They could get the raw materials to build these solar cells by mining the surface of the Moon.

Work on smaller space platforms began in the 1960s. Scientists working for the United States Air Force were first to suggest an actual plan to build a habitat in space. It was called the Manned Orbital Laboratory (MOL) and would have been built inside the shell of a Titan rocket. The plan was to launch astronauts to the MOL in a Gemini-type capsule. The astronauts would have lived on board MOL for a month at a time, using telescopes to look down on Earth and watch the military operations of other countries. Soon, however, robotic telescopes were designed for these missions, and the Air Force cancelled the program after just one unmanned test launch.

Soviet space engineers also developed a habitat like MOL. It was called *Salyut,* and it had about as much room as a small motor home. At least 10 were eventually built, and the first, called *Salyut 1*, was launched April 19, 1971. Cosmonaut Viktor Ivanovich Patsaev was the first human to climb aboard a space station when he and two other cosmonauts rocketed to *Salyut 1* in a Soyuz capsule. Some of the Salyuts were used for military missions, the rest for scientific research.

Challenges

There are some important medical problems involved in living in space for longer than a few days. Because persons in space don't feel the force of gravity, they gradually lose strength in their bones and muscles. After a few months in space, there is a risk that astronauts won't be able to recover their strength when they return to Earth. Medical experts learned that vigorous exercise helps keep the human body healthy in space, so any modern space station includes exercise equipment similar to what is used in a school gym.

NASA eventually built something similar to the MOL in the 1970s, using an empty rocket booster as a space station. It was originally called the Orbital Workshop, but it became known as *Skylab.* Originally the plan was to use a working rocket booster and rebuild it from the inside after the fuel was consumed in the launch. However, the *Saturn V* rocket was so powerful that it could boost *Skylab* directly into orbit, even without the extra fuel. So, it was possible to send *Skylab* already fitted out for astronauts to live in it. Three teams of three astronauts each were sent up to *Skylab.* The first team had to perform some difficult but important repair work to fix *Skylab's* sunlight shield and solar power cells, but the project was very successful by the time *Skylab* was closed.

The next logical step was to assemble a space habitat out of separate modules that could be launched like *Salyut* or *Skylab*. Seven separate modules were launched by the Soviet Union, beginning in 1986, to build *Mir*. In total, *Mir* was about as big as a school classroom, divided into smaller sections by the individual modules. Dozens of cosmonauts—and seven astronauts from the United States—spent many months living on *Mir*. When the

SERGEI KRIKALEV

In 2005, Sergei Konstantinovich Krikalev made his sixth trip into orbit around Earth. Living aboard the International Space Station, Krikalev set the record for more total time in space than any other astronaut—more than 800 days! He has now traveled farther than any human being in history. After studying to be an engineer in the former Soviet Union, Krikalev worked on the Soviet space shuttle project that was cancelled, spent time aboard *Mir*, and became the first Russian cosmonaut to fly on the United States space shuttle. He has also performed almost a dozen space walks.

It wasn't easy for Krikalev, who was born in St. Petersburg, to adjust to life in Texas when he first came to work for NASA. But now he even has a fan club! Perhaps Krikalev will get a chance to walk on the Moon some day.

Sergei Krikalev has spent more than two years in space—803 days, 9 hours, and 39 minutes, to be exact.

The modular *Mir* space station was built by the former Soviet Union and spent 15 years in orbit.

political situation changed, and Russia took over the space projects of the former Soviet Union, plans for a second *Mir* space platform were dropped.

A Ferry to Space

Meanwhile, NASA had plans to start building a modular habitat similar to *Mir*. After *Skylab*, NASA wanted to stop using space capsules that could only go into space and return to Earth once. The idea of a reusable plane that could be launched into space on a rocket but land on a regular runway turned into the space shut-

Punching through the clouds, the space shuttle *Columbia* was launched on mission STS-47 in 1992.

tle. Its first flight was in 1981, and more than 110 successful missions have already taken place. Like any form of space travel, danger is never far away. There have been two deadly catastrophes in which the space shuttles *Challenger* and *Columbia* were destroyed. NASA plans to fly the remaining three space shuttles— *Atlantis, Endeavor,* and *Discovery*—at least until 2010.

The space shuttle has a cargo bay about the size of a bus. Its purpose is to carry different kinds of hardware into orbit around Earth, such as the Hubble Space Telescope, and even rockets that can fire after they are released from the cargo bay and travel farther into the solar system. However, the most important payload that the space shuttle was built to carry is the modules for the space station that NASA wanted to build.

The International Space Station
International cooperation in space enjoyed a dramatic moment as early as 1975, when NASA and the former Soviet Union linked an Apollo capsule and a Soyuz in orbit around Earth. Then, the

This cutaway drawing shows astronauts and cosmonauts shaking hands on the Apollo-Soyuz cooperative space mission.

Soviet Union split into separate countries, and NASA had the opportunity to form a partnership with Russia. So, NASA's plan for a space habitat was merged with the proposals for a second *Mir*, and a more ambitious project began. It was called the International Space Station (ISS). When the space shuttle *Endeavour* brought the *Unity* module to space and connected it to the Russian-built *Zarya* module in December 1998, the ISS was born. It was designed so that both the Russian *Soyuz* spacecraft and the U.S. space shuttle could dock there. When it is completed, there will be more than a dozen modules and structures incorporated into the ISS.

Dozens of astronauts have lived there already. Other countries, such as Brazil, Canada, Italy, and Japan, have also joined the global effort. *Skylab*, the *Salyuts* and *Mir* have all re-entered and burned up in the atmosphere, so the ISS is now the world's only space station. It is the largest object humans have yet put in outer space. Even though it may be many years before there are cities in space, we can say that the permanent occupation of space by human beings has already begun.

CHAPTER NINE

Private Space

Space exploration is very expensive. Much of the cost is related to the strict safety standards for hardware used in space. Another reason is simply that so much fuel is needed to lift anything up so high and get it moving fast enough to stay in orbit. There are different fuels available for a rocket designer to choose from, but some require more expensive handling or larger fuel tanks.

In 2000, it cost anywhere from $2,000 to $20,000 per pound to launch a traditional rocket. NASA's space shuttle was originally designed to be less expensive than rocket launches in the 1960s. Yet, it has always been more expensive than the traditional rockets. In 2000, it still cost between $100 million and $500 million to launch a space shuttle.

Competition in Space

NASA gets billions of dollars from the United States government. But there are some private companies that plan to make a profitable business out of space exploration. Most of them have built rockets that carry only cargo, not astronauts. Then, a $10 million prize was offered for the first spaceship that could carry a person to the edge of outer space twice in two weeks. Called the Ansari

Burt Rutan poses casually with a parrot perched on his shoulder. Even years before winning the Ansari X Prize, Rutan was known for his ingenious and successful aircraft designs.

X Prize, this competition fired up the imagination of more than 20 teams in different countries. It was inspired by aviation prizes, like the one that encouraged Charles Lindbergh to make the first solo flight in an airplane from New York to Paris in 1927.

One of the engineers who got excited about the Ansari X Prize was Burt Rutan. Rutan and his company in California were famous for designing unconventional aircraft. About the competition to reach space, Rutan said, "We need affordable space travel to inspire our youth, to let them know that they can lead all of us to future progress in exploration, discovery, and fun."

Rutan's team chose a two-stage, piggyback system for their Ansari X Prize entry. Both stages have wings for regular flight in the atmosphere. The first stage, called *White Knight*, is powered by jet engines and has room for a pilot and two passengers. After a traditional takeoff from a runway, *White Knight* carries the rocket stage to an altitude of 50,000 feet (15,000 m), releases the rocket stage, and then returns to a safe landing on the same runway from which it took off.

The rocket stage is called *SpaceShipOne* and is about 16 feet (5 m) long, with a similar wingspan. Multiple round windows and a sharp nose make it look like a science fiction design from the 1950s. But it is made out of high-tech plastic materials and sports a rocket motor that burns for just a few minutes. When the rocket motor runs out of fuel, *SpaceShipOne* continues to climb to just over 60 miles (100,000 m). On the way back down from the near-perfect vacuum of space, the back half of the wings fold up to prevent *SpaceShipOne* from losing control as the atmosphere gets thicker. *SpaceShipOne* then lands on a runway under the pilot's control, just like a regular glider.

Winning the X Prize

After more than 50 test flights of *White Knight* and *SpaceShipOne*, Rutan's team was ready to try for the $10 million prize. They made a flight of 64.2 miles (103 km) and were ready to make the second flight, as required by the Ansari X Prize rules, on October 4, 2004. On that morning, high above the Mojave Desert, astro-

THE SKYLON SPACE PLANE

A completely reusable rocket would cost less to launch. One way to make a rocket completely reusable is called Single Stage to Orbit (SSTO). This means that the entire rocket would go all the way into space, without dropping any fuel tank or rocket stages.

A possible design for an SSTO spacecraft is called *Skylon*. It is a space plane that would rely on oxygen from the air until it was going at hypersonic speed, which is about 3,300 miles per hour (5,400 km/h) and burning rocket fuel at even faster speeds. It would carry cargo but no astronauts. So far, the *Skylon* project is still on the drawing board, but scientists and engineers in Great Britain are working to solve the challenges involved.

Canadian Arrow is a company in Canada that was inspired by the Ansari X Prize. They are building a rocket that would fly paying customers to the edge of space. With a simple, two-stage design, *Canadian Arrow* is 54 feet (16 m) tall. It would be launched over the Great Lakes and land in water. Although the *Canadian Arrow* rocket would not go into orbit, the altitude of about 62.5 miles (100 km) would qualify it as a trip into space. Even though *SpaceShipOne* has already won the Ansari X Prize, the Canadian Arrow team has continued developing their rocket.

They hope to become a successful business—a sort of space tourist agency. For a price under $100,000, a tourist could go through a two-week training course at the Canadian Arrow Space Center and then take a 20-minute flight on the rocket. A really adventurous person could even jump out of the rocket capsule and space dive back to the ground. Some years ago, Burt Rutan said, "We will have space tourism where you will

Computer artwork shows a fanciful launch from a possible lunar base.

be able to see the black sky and the curvature of the Earth. It will be the most exciting roller coaster ride you can buy." The 7-Up soft drink company has promised to give away a trip into space some day.

Slung under *White Knight*, *SpaceShipOne* was carried upward on this flight, the first of two required by the Ansari X Prize rules.

naut Brian Binnie released from White Knight and took the rocket into space to a new record altitude of 69.6 miles (112 km). The record was verified by radar instruments on the ground. It was official: The Ansari X Prize was theirs. *SpaceShipOne* has now been retired to the Smithsonian Institution's Air and Space Museum.

KEY DISCOVERIES ABOUT SPACE

These lists highlight key moments, breakthroughs, and tools in the field of space exploration.

Great Moments in Human Space Exploration
- Launch of the first liquid-fueled rocket, 1926
- Launch of *Sputnik*, the first human artifact in orbit around Earth, 1957
- Launch of Yuri Gagarin, first person to orbit Earth, 1961
- First space walk, 1965
- First docking of two spacecraft, 1966
- First landing on the Moon, 1969
- Handshake between Tom Stafford and Alexei Leonov on *Apollo-Soyuz*, 1975
- First launch of the space shuttle *Columbia*, 1981
- Docking of *Kvant 1* with the *Mir* core module, forming the first space station, 1987
- Flight of *SpaceShipOne* to win the Ansari X Prize, 2004

This footprint on the Moon represents a small step into the cosmos but a giant leap for all humanity.

Great Moments in Robotic Space Exploration
- *Luna 3*'s first photographs of the Moon's far side, 1959
- *Mariner 4*'s photographs of craters on Mars, 1965
- The first data from the atmosphere of Venus by *Venera 4*, 1967
- The first data from surface of Venus by *Venera 4*, 1970
- *Mariner 10*'s photographs of craters on Mercury, 1975
- The Landing of *Viking 1* on Mars, 1976
- The first pictures of volcanoes on Io by *Voyager 1*, 1979
- *Voyager 2*'s first photographs of Neptune's blue atmosphere, 1989
- *Galileo*'s photographs of the crash of comet Shoemaker-Levy 9 into Jupiter, 1994
- *Huygens*' first photographs from surface of Titan, 2005

An artist drew this picture of one of the rovers that was sent to explore Mars in 2004.

Great Breakthroughs in Astronomy

- Discovery of precession by Hipparchus, about 130 B.C.
- Second Law of Orbital Motion by Johannes Kepler, 1609
- Discovery of the moons of Jupiter by Galileo Galilei, 1610
- Return of Halley's comet as predicted, 1758
- Discovery of Uranus by William Herschel, 1781
- List of dark lines in the colors of the Sun by Joseph Fraunhofer, 1814
- Location of the center of the Milky Way galaxy by Harlow Shapley, 1917
- Measurement of the expansion of the universe by Edwin Hubble, 1929
- Detection of cosmic microwave background radiation, 1964
- Photographs of the impact of comet Shoemaker-Levy 9 into Jupiter, 1994

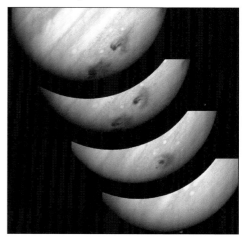

Shown here are four different stages of the awesome impacts of Comet Shoemaker-Levy 9 on Jupiter during a few days in 1994.

Biggest Telescopes on Earth

(The size of the **aperture** is given, along with the location of the telescope.)

- South African Large Telescope, 36 feet (11 m), South Africa
- Great Telescope of the Canary Islands, 34 feet (10.4 m), Spain
- Keck I and Keck II, both 33 feet (10 m), Hawaii
- Hobby-Eberly Telescope, 30 feet (9.2 m), Texas
- Large Binocular Telescope, each scope 27 feet (8.3 m), Arizona
- Subaru, 27 feet (8.3 m), Hawaii
- Very Large Telescope-1, VLT-2, VLT-3, and VLT-4, 26.9 feet (8.2 m), Chile
- Gemini North (Hawaii) and Gemini South (Chile), each 26.6 feet (8.1 m)
- Multiple Mirror Telescope, 21 feet (6.5 m), Arizona
- Magellan I and Magellan II, each 21 feet (6.5 m), Chile

The Keck I observatory has the largest telescope in the United States.

Glossary

aperture – the size of the opening at the front of a telescope that lets in the light; usually the same size as the main mirror or lens

apogee – the farthest point that a satellite reaches in its orbit around Earth

asteroid – an object in space, smaller than a planet, that orbits the Sun and is mostly rocky

astronaut – a person who has been in outer space. According to the U.S. Federal Aviation Authority, if you fly to an altitude of 328,000 feet (100,000 m), you are considered an astronaut.

ballistic – the flight or motion of an object, such as a rocket or a bullet, through air or space after whatever force propelled it has stopped pushing

big bang – the explosion that started the universe 13,700,000,000 years ago

blueberries – tiny, round, gray rocks on the surface of Mars, which contain hematite, a mineral that is usually formed in water; discovered by the Opportunity rover

celestial mechanics – the rules that govern the motion of objects through space, mainly under the influence of each other's gravity

Clarke orbit an orbit around Earth at an altitude of 22,300 miles (36,000 km), which is geosynchronous because a satellite takes exactly the same time to orbit Earth as Earth's rotation, 24 hours

cosmonaut – the Russian word for "astronaut"

dock – to bring two spacecraft together in outer space and connect them so that passengers or anything else can be transferred between them

microwaves – a type of energy that can be sent through air or space. Microwaves are similar to radio waves or light, but invisible.

NASA – (National Aeronautics and Space Administration) the department of the United States government that is responsible for all nonmilitary research and development in outer space

nebula – any faraway object that has the appearance of a small cloud in a telescope. Since these were first discovered, many have turned out to be swarms of stars, but some are truly vast clouds of gas in space.

nuclear weapon – a device that uses energy from the nucleus of atoms either for destructive explosive force or to spread danger over a wide area

orbit – the path of any natural or artificial satellite in space as it travels around a larger object under the influence of gravity

payload – cargo or passengers or anything else that is carried up by a rocket except for the fuel and the rocket equipment itself

perigee – the point in a satellite's orbit around Earth when the satellite and Earth are closest together

radar – a technology based on transmitting radio waves and then receiving their echoes. Radar is used in space exploration to measure the distance and texture of the surfaces of objects up to millions of miles (km) away.

radioisotope thermoelectric generator – (RTG) a device that uses nuclear reactions to generate heat and electricity, mainly used on spacecraft that will travel too far from the Sun to use solar energy

re-entry – the return of a spaceship from outer space to Earth's atmosphere, ending with a landing either in the water or on land

refractor – a type of telescope that has a clear lens at the front to collect faint light

reflector – a type of telescope that has a curved mirror at the back to collect faint light

rendezvous – a close approach of two spacecraft or other objects that do not quite touch each other in space

rocket – a vehicle that propels itself by combustion of fuel and oxygen, both of which are carried by the rocket itself

thermocouple – an electronic device designed to turn heat into electricity

trajectory – the path of a rocket or any other vehicle through air or space

Bibliography

Armstrong, Neil, Aldrin, Edwin, and Collins, Michael. *First on the Moon*. Boston: Little, Brown & Company, 1970.

Chaikin, Andrew. *A Man on the Moon*. New York: Penguin Books, 1999.

Chaikin, Andrew. *Space*. London, UK: Carlton Books, 2002.

Collins, Michael. *Carrying the Fire*. New York: Farrar, Straus and Giroux, 1974.

Cortright, Edgar, Editor. "Apollo Expeditions to the Moon," NASA SP-350. Washington: National Aeronautics and Space Administration, 1975.

Footprints on the Moon, companion to the television documentary: www.abc.net.au/science/moon/footprints.htm

Glossary of space terminology: www.braeunig.us/space/glossary.htm

Hermann Oberth Space Museum: www.oberth-museum.org/index_e.html

History of space exploration: www.solarviews.com/eng/history.htm

History of Space Travel: http://my.execpc.com/~culp/space/history.html

Jet Propulsion Laboratory home page: www.jpl.nasa.gov

McNamara, Bernard. *Into the Final Frontier: The Human Exploration of Space*. Philadelphia: Harcourt College Publishers, 2001.

Miller, Ron, and Hartmann, William K. *The Grand Tour: A Traveler's Guide to the Solar System*. New York: Workman Press, 1993.

National Aeronautics and Space Administration historical resources: www.nasa.gov/missions/past/index.html

Sergei Korolov: http://www.korolev.ru/english/e_biografia.html

Summerlin, Lee, Editor. "Skylab, Classroom in Space," NASA SP-401. Washington: National Aeronautics and Space Administration, 1977.

Wilford, John Noble. *We Reach the Moon*. New York: Bantam Books, 1969.

Wolfe, Tom. *The Right Stuff*. New York: Farrar, Straus and Giroux, 1979.

Yuri Gagarin biography: www.tdf.it/numero1/yg_bio.htm

Further Exploration

BOOKS

Ashby, Ruth, *Rocket Man: The Mercury Adventure of John Glenn.* Atlanta, Ga.: Peachtree, 2004.

Asimov, Isaac, *Piloted Space Flights.* Milwaukee, Wis.: G. Stevens, 1990.

Mason, Paul, *The Space Race.* Austin, Tex.: Raintree Steck-Vaughn, 2002.

Reichhardt, Tony, editor, *Space Shuttle: The First 20 Years.* Washington D.C.: Smithsonian Institution; London: DK Publishing, 2002.

Schyffert, Bea Uusma, *The Man Who Went to the Far Side of the Moon: The Story of Apollo 11 Astronaut Michael Collins.* San Francisco, Calif.: Chronicle Books, 2003.

Somervill, Barbara A. *The History of Space Travel.* Chanhassen, Minn.: The Child's World, 2005.

Stille, Darlene R., *Space Shuttle.* Minneapolis, Minn.: Compass Point Books, 2004.

Stott, Carole, *Space Exploration.* New York: DK Publishing, 2004.

WEB SITES

www.jpl.nasa.gov/basics
Basics of Space Flight

www.braeunig.us/space/glossary.html
Glossary

www.solarviews.com/eng/rocket.html
History of rocketry

www.solarviews.com/eng/history.html
History of space exploration

www.qrg.northwestern.edu/projects/vss/docs/space-environment/zoom-travel.html
How do objects in space travel?

www.astrophys-assist.com/educate/spaceflight/spaceflight.html
Human spaceflight

www.hq.nasa.gov/osf/ISS_Configuration.pdf
International space station components

www.nasa.gov/images/content/116932main_mol_full.jpg
Manned orbiting laboratory

www.reactionengines.co.uk
Skylon SSTO

www.delta.edu/planet/teacher_mats/spacecraft.html
Solar system exploration missions

www.heavens-above.com/solar-escape.asp
Spacecraft escaping the solar system

lunar.arc.nasa.gov/education/teacher
Teacher's guide to the Moon

ulysses-ops.jpl.esa.int/ulsfct/rgpCafe/solsys/solsys.html
Where is the Ulysses spacecraft?

Index

Page numbers for illustrations are in *italic*

About the Author

PETER JEDICKE teaches mathematics and science at Fanshawe College in London, Canada. He has studied physics and philosophy, and is an active amateur astronomer, involved both locally and nationally in the Royal Astronomical Society of Canada. Jedicke has written articles for *Astronomy* magazine and *Sky & Telescope* magazine. His other books include *Cosmology: Exploring the Universe, SETI: The Search for Alien Intelligence,* and *Scientific American's The Big Idea.*

Picture Credits